I0606214

DISCOVER ANCIENT CIVILIZATIONS

Ancient China

by M.J. York

CAPSTONE VALUE LIBRARY
a capstone imprint

Published by Capstone® Value Library, an imprint of Capstone
1710 Roe Crest Drive, North Mankato, Minnesota 56003
capstonepub.com

Library of Congress Cataloging-in-Publication Data is available on the Library of Congress website
ISBN: 9798875306730 (hardcover)
ISBN: 9798875306761 (ebook PDF)

Summary: An exploration of the history and legacy of ancient China.

Editorial Credits
Editor: Kellie M. Hultgren; Designer: Jennifer Walker; Production Specialist: Tori Abraham

Image Credits
Dreamstime: Flysea, 21, Mengzhang, 23, Sean Pavone, cover, Shengguangping Sheng, 5, Tatiana Kashko, 7, Tsangming Chang, 9, Vyychan, 13; Shutterstock: Javen, 17

Printed and bound in the USA. 006585

Table of Contents

CHAPTER 1

Ancient China

China is a huge and ancient land. Its civilization has lasted for more than 4,000 years. In many ways it continues today. Legends tell of Huangdi, the Yellow Emperor. He lived in the 2600s BCE. He united the people who lived around the Yellow River.

Ancient China was located in the heart of modern China. Its borders often changed. Emperors expanded their control. But with disasters or uprisings, the empire shrunk again.

The land was good for growing food, and people usually lived well. They made beautiful works of art. They invented silk, gunpowder, paper, printing, and more.

The Yellow River got its name from the color of the muddy silt in the water.

CHAPTER 2

Rivers and Rain

Chinese culture began on the Yellow River. The valley had rich soil. Farming was easy. But there were often floods or droughts. China's other major river is the Yangtze. It is the longest river in Asia.

A rain belt cuts across China from north to south. **Monsoons** wet the land to the east. To the west it is drier. There are mountains and deserts.

Nomads from the west often attacked the farmlands to the east. The Great Wall of China partially follows the rain belt, where crops grow best. Its purpose was protecting the farmland from attack. But it could not stop all **invasions**.

The city of Gaochang was built in the first century BCE on the edge of the Taklamakan Desert. Only ruins remain.

CHAPTER 3

Dynasties and Emperors

Writing and **artifacts** tell the story of many ruling **dynasties**. The earliest dynasty with written records is the Shang (1600 to 1050 BCE).

In 221 BCE, Emperor Qin conquered several warring states. This unified China into one empire. His **imperial** system lasted with few interruptions until 1912 CE.

The emperor was at the top of Chinese society. His family and close advisers made up his court. They all lived in the palace. The emperor led a highly organized government. It sent orders to the **provinces**. There, local officials made sure the emperor's orders were followed.

An emperor of the Han dynasty ordered this section of the Great Wall built in northern China in 121 BCE.

The government also made laws. Leaders thought people needed laws so they would behave. Laws had to be strict and enforced equally for everyone. This way of thinking is called legalism.

The Han Dynasty and Confucianism

The Han dynasty began around 202 BCE and lasted more than 400 years. Emperor Wu of Han decided the government should follow Confucianism.

The **philosopher** Confucius lived earlier, in the 500s to 400s BCE. He hoped for harmony and peace in China. He wanted to return to older ways of life. He believed each person had a role in society. Everyone had responsibilities to others. People should treat each other with kindness.

Government workers of the Han dynasty took tests on Confucianism. They studied at a college in the capital city. This system lasted for centuries.

CHAPTER 4

Daily Life

Ancient homes were built of wood. Few traces remain today. But clay models found in tombs tell us more. Homes had pointed roofs protected by tiles. Roof decorations became more elaborate over time.

Food was considered medicine. It was part of **rituals** and celebrations. People believed each food had its own benefits. They tried to eat the right balance to be healthy.

Around the time of Emperor Qin, farmers grew a lot of wheat. People ate noodles, dumplings, bread, and steamed buns. Tea was grown first as a medicine and later as a drink.

The soldiers and horses lined up in Emperor Qin's tomb are made of terra-cotta clay.

Science and the Military

Chinese scientists invented a compass using magnets by the Han dynasty. They were causing explosions with gunpowder by the 900s CE. They used advanced math and engineering to build grand palaces and strong bridges.

Military power was important to the empire. We know much about ancient Chinese armies because of Emperor Qin's tomb. It held thousands of life-size clay statues of soldiers and horses. Each soldier has a different face. They were once brightly painted. They show what armor, swords, bows and arrows, and chariots were like then.

CHAPTER 6

Living a Good Life

Ancient Chinese beliefs honor the ancestors, ghosts, and many gods. Believers make offerings and perform rituals. One traditional celebration is the Spring Festival, or Lunar New Year. Hanging red lanterns and shooting fireworks bring luck. Confucianism also calls for honoring the ancestors.

Taoism helps followers live in balance with nature. They follow Tao, or "the way," to take right actions. Often taking no action is the right course. The *Tao Te Ching* was written in the 500s BCE. It holds Taoism's central teachings.

Buddhism came to China in the first century CE. Buddhists follow the teachings of the holy man Buddha. They believe souls are reborn again after death. Every action, good or bad, is later paid back.

These ideas about living a good life wove together over time. People combined pieces from each tradition in their beliefs and daily lives.

A stone carving from the Eastern Han period (25–220 CE) shows a legendary meeting between Confucius and Laozi, the founder of Taoism.

CHAPTER 7

The Legacy of China

Chinese inventions and **exports** changed the world. Silk, tea, gunpowder, and paper traveled far beyond the empire's borders.

Many parts of ancient China are still alive and vibrant today. Tourists walk the Great Wall and view Emperor Qin's pottery warriors each year. Traditional medicine, clothing, religion, and literature are part of everyday life. Elegant calligraphy, fine arts and crafts, and stunning architecture draw from the past as they look to the future.

Children practice traditional Chinese calligraphy with brushes and ink.

Glossary

artifacts (AR-tuh-faktz)—objects remaining from an earlier time

calligraphy (kuh-LI-gruh-fee)—artistic or stylized writing; Chinese calligraphy is a form of art created with a brush and ink

dynasties (DYE-nuh-steez)—ruling families with related people holding power one after the other

exports (EK-sports)—goods sold away from a country or region

imperial (im-PIHR-ee-uhl)—having to do with an emperor or empire

invasions (in-VEY-zhnz)—attacks from armies or enemies crossing the borders of a country or region

lacquerware (LAK-ur-wehr)—things made of wood painted with thin layers of a plastic-like tree sap

monsoons (mon-SOONZ)—seasons of heavy rainfall

nomads (NOH-madz)—groups of people who travel throughout a region rather than having one fixed spot to live

philosopher (fuh-LOSS-uh-fur)—person who seeks wisdom and understanding

provinces (PROV-uhn-suhz)—regions into which a larger country or kingdom is divided

rituals (RICH-oo-uhlz)—established forms, actions, or words of a ceremony

Index